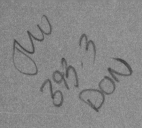

If a Mummy Could Talk . . .

by Rhonda Lucas Donald   Illustrated by Cathy Morrison

Lyuba

Siberia, 42,000 years ago

Hi, I'm Lyuba (LOO-buh), a baby woolly mammoth. My shaggy fur coat keeps me warm here in the Arctic. One day, I'll grow to be as big as Momma. But I'm only one month old now. It's spring, and ice is melting all over. Momma just fed me a nice milk meal. Now we're going exploring along the riverbank. Come on. Let's go!

Facts about Lyuba from Dr. Daniel Fisher

Lyuba is the size of a large dog. In her tummy were the remains of milk from her last meal. Besides the milk was plant pollen.

Sadly, little Lyuba's life ended when she fell through the ice over a lake and sank to the bottom. Her trunk, mouth, and lungs were filled with mud that choked the baby. A reindeer herder and his sons found her body, still frozen, in 2007.

Lyuba is a Russian word for love.

Blue Babe, Steppe Bison

Alaska, 36,000 Years Ago

The weather is getting colder, and the grazing is getting thinner. Winter is coming. But I'm used to that. Sniff. SNIFF! What's that? I'm not the only one looking for a meal. Smells like a lion. Better hoof it!

Facts about Babe from R. Dale Guthrie

Gold miners found Babe's mummy in 1979. It is a steppe bison, an extinct type of bison that lived during the last Ice Age. The body was so well preserved that you could see claw and teeth wounds from an American lion. So it appears that the lion won this struggle. But it grew cold so fast that the bison's body froze and prevented it from being eaten.

A **steppe** is a large area of flat grassland in Siberia.

Otzi, the Ice Man

Ouch! My teeth are giving me fits. Plus I've got plenty of other aches and pains. No wonder after that fight the other day. I'm laying low up here in the hills. It's spring, and there's plenty to eat. Think I'll work on my bow some. It's not yet finished. Might need it if those fellas come back.

Facts about Otzi from Dr. Albert Zink

Otzi is the victim of a very old murder mystery. He was shot with an arrow minutes before his death. A day or two before, he may have been in a fight and suffered wounds to the hand and head. Otzi had clothing, tools, and a copper ax. Tattoos on his arms, legs, and back may have marked spots for acupuncture, an ancient form of medicine.

King Tut

Egypt, 3,300 years ago

Hand me my cane, mortal. Can't get around without it or my special shoes. I've never been in the best of health. But as pharaoh, I am still god on Earth. *Bzzzzzz.* SMACK! Ugh, can't anyone get rid of these pesky mosquitoes?

Facts about Tut from Dr. Albert Zink

Tut's mummy has numerous broken bones. The latest computer scans show that only one injury happened before Tut died: a broken leg. But the boy king had many health problems. He had malaria (a sickness carried by mosquitoes) and probably had a club foot. He would have needed a cane to walk. DNA tests showed that his parents were likely brother and sister.

A **club foot** is when someone's foot turns in, making it difficult to walk.

Ramesses III

Egypt, more than 3,000 years ago

I am the pharaoh, and I demand justice! My wives are up to something. And I don't think I can trust one of my sons either. You'd think that ruling for 30 years and protecting Egypt from invaders three times would get me some respect. What a pain in the neck.

Facts about Ramesses from Dr. Albert Zink

Scientists wondered what might be beneath the thick layer of bandages around the neck of Ramesses III's mummy. Scans showed a deep cut from a sharp knife that could easily have killed him. But one of his toes was also cut off by a heavy blade like an ax. That may mean he was attacked by more than one person. Documents of trials at the time say that some of the pharaoh's many wives plotted to kill him. His son Pentawere was tried for his murder and found guilty.

Pharaoh's Dog
Egypt, more than 3,000 years ago

I'm one lucky pup! As the pet of the pharaoh, I am hand-fed only the tastiest treats. I get to go everywhere with him. I will even be buried here in a special tomb (along with my master's pet baboon). Cats might think they're special, but I'm the pharaoh's favorite. Oh boy, looks like we're going hunting!

Facts about the dog mummy from Dr. Salima Ikram

This dog has lost its bandages but is still well preserved. It was a hunting dog that probably belonged to a pharaoh. That's how it ended up as a mummy in its own tomb in the Valley of the Kings. Ikram says the dog "would have been fed nibbly bits and spoiled rotten." That describes a lot of pets today!

Cat Mummy

Egypt, 3,000 years ago

It's a zoo around here! I've never seen so many animals in one place. Some of us are beloved pets. Some, like me, are companions of the gods. Some poor critters are offerings. These Egyptians make mummies out of anybody! Ooo—sorry momma croc. Don't mind me. I won't bother your babies.

Facts about animal mummies from Dr. Salima Ikram

Egyptians mummified animals for four main reasons. They might have been pets to keep their owners company in the afterlife. Others provided food for the dead. Some animals were revered as gods themselves. Others were offerings. In modern times, large numbers of animal mummies have been destroyed. They were even used as fertilizer.

Tamut
Ancient Egypt, 2,900 years ago

La, la, la, la, LAHHH. Just warming up my voice. I've sung in the best temples in Luxor, you know. Temple life is good. People bring the very best foods for the god Amun. And I get to eat them!

Like any star, I have my secrets. Whatever it takes for fame to live on! See you in the afterlife. Maybe you'll get to hear me sing someday.

Facts about Tamut from Dr. John Taylor and scientists at the British Museum

Tamut was a chantress or temple singer. How do we know? Writing (hieroglyphs) on her sarcophagus (casket) tells us. Tamut was buried with many jewels and even artificial eyes. They were to help her see in the afterlife.

CT scans revealed her features, the bling, and a clue about her health. One of her arteries was clogged. The scientists say they may soon be able to recreate what Tamut's voice might have sounded like. Bet she's a bit rusty after nearly 3,000 years!

Tollund Man
Denmark, 2,300–2,400 years ago

I've been digging peat in this bog my whole life. So I guess it's fitting that I end up here in the end. We farmers are at the mercy of the gods and the weather they bring. Lately it's been soggy and cold—no good for crops. So I'm ready for what comes . . . I think.

Facts about Tollund Man from Silkeborg Museum

Tollund Man is one of the best-preserved prehistoric bodies ever found. He was found in a peat bog, where he was gently laid after being hanged. Experts believe he was a sacrifice to the bog. Most bodies at the time would have been burned.

Lady Dai
China, 2,200 years ago

Yes, I must have those silks. And my face powders. Don't forget the musicians! I don't want to leave anything behind. After all, the afterlife should be as glorious as life is. But preparing for the afterlife is tiring. I think I'll have a little snack. Care for some melon?

Facts about Lady Dai from Willow Weilan Hai Chang

Lady Dai was the wife of a regional ruler of China. She was rich and led a privileged life. She and her family were mummified and placed in a deep tomb. Inside the tomb were 1,000 precious possessions. Her mummy is one of the best preserved ever found. Her skin was still moist!

Inca Maiden

Argentina, 500 years ago

I was nervous when they chose me to be a sacrifice to the gods. But it is an honor, right? I don't have much time to think about it. For a year, my two young friends and I travel all over. We are famous! Until my day comes and we climb the great mountain, I get to eat the best foods and chew coca leaves. So relaxing . . .

Facts about the Inca Maiden
from Dr. Johan Reinhard

Johan Reinhard and his team found the Inca Maiden and her two young companions frozen atop an Andean mountain in 1999. She was about 13 at the time of her death, and the younger children were about four. She was buried in the frozen earth, which preserved her body so well that she appears to have simply fallen asleep. Her hair was still neatly braided in long strands.

Vladimir Lenin

Russia, 1924

Changing the country isn't easy. It took years, and millions died in our cause. But Russia will be a workers' paradise if it kills me! An assassin tried to do that a few years ago. Hah! I'm still here, even if I'm not such a young man anymore. My, the winters in Moscow seem to get colder every year.

Facts about Lenin from Dr. Alexei Yurchak

Lenin died in 1924 during the Russian winter. The cold helped preserve his body while it was on display for millions of mourners. Joseph Stalin ordered that Lenin's body be preserved, and hundreds of scientists have maintained the body ever since. Unlike other mummies, Lenin's body isn't wrapped. A mix of chemicals and periodic cleaning keep the body looking good. The body isn't exactly "original," though. All of his internal organs were removed. Skin, eyelashes, and body fat have been replaced with plastic and other artificial materials.

For Creative Minds

This section may be photocopied or printed from our website by the owner of this book for educational, non-commercial use. Cross-curricular teaching activities for use at home or in the classroom, interactive quizzes, and more are available online.

Visit www.ArbordalePublishing.com to explore additional resources.

Mummy Map

Mummy	Country	Continent
Blue Babe	USA	North America
Inca Maiden	Argentina	South America
Tamut	Egypt	Africa
Lady Dai	China	Asia
Otzi	Italy	Europe

There are mummies all over the world. Which of these mummies was found closest to where you live?

1. Which ocean is closest to Blue Babe?
2. Which mummy is south of Otzi?
3. Which ocean is closest to Lady Dai?

4. Which ocean is closest to the Inca Maiden?
5. Which two mummies are in the Americas?
6. Which mummy is east of Tamut?

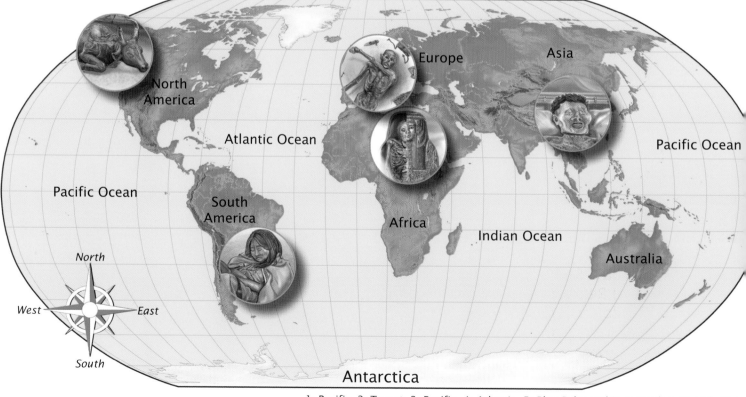

1: Pacific. 2: Tamut. 3: Pacific. 4: Atlantic. 5: Blue Babe and Inca Maiden. 6: Lady Dai

Mummy Scientists and Their Tools

Scientists who study ancient human artifacts and remains such as the mummy of King Tut are archaeologists. Scientists who study the remains of ancient plants and animals like Lyuba are paleontologists. Both use similar methods and tools to locate sites, objects, and remains to study. By analyzing fossils, preserved remains, and the artifacts surrounding them, they can piece together something of how the person or animal lived and died.

An artifact is an object made by people.

Tools and Technology

Scientists use medical scanning equipment to "see" inside fossils and mummies. These are some of the tools researchers use:

DNA	DNA can show family relations (such as Ramesses III and his son) and can expose diseases the person or animal might have had.
CT Scan	A computer combines multiple x-rays in layers to make a 3-D cross-section of bones and soft tissues.
MRI	Magnetic field and radio waves produce 3-D images of organs and tissues.
X-ray	Radiation passes through the body. Denser structures such as bone show up better on an X-ray than soft tissues.
Chemical tests	Chemicals in the body can show what the mummy ate, what certain materials are made of, or the presence of disease.

Do you want to be an archaeologist or paleontologist? It takes many years of study and field experience, but if you work hard the dream can come true! Most archaeologists and paleontologists get advanced college degrees in their field of study. But you can prepare even before starting college! Read as much about the field as possible. Volunteer to help research at a museum, or work on a dig. This will help you develop the skills and experience you need to start your science career!

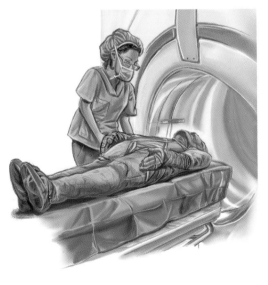

How to Make a Mummy

There are several ways to make a mummy. Here are the four main ways mummies get preserved.

Bogged Down

Tollund Man and other bog mummies were preserved in a wet environment. While this seems like it would rot the bodies faster, the water in a peat bog has very little oxygen. Bacteria that cause a body to decay need oxygen to survive. And bog water is acidic. It's like mild vinegar, which can help preserve canned food. Just like vinegar turns a cucumber into a pickle, the chemistry of bog water "pickles" a body.

Drying Out

The first mummies were made naturally. Dry conditions like those in a desert will naturally preserve a body. The Egyptians must have realized this in perfecting their method of mummification. But they weren't the only ones. Along the western coast of South America, the climate is dry and the soil contains salts that helped preserve bodies. Here bodies were buried in the sand to dry them before they were tied together in a seated position and wrapped in layers of cloth. Prized possessions were tucked into pouches and hung on the body.

Egyptian Method

The Egyptians' elaborate process of mummification could take more than two months to complete. First, the body's organs were removed, including the brain, which was sometimes pulled out through the nose with hooks. The organs were preserved in canopic jars. Sometimes the heart was left inside the body. Egyptians believed the gods would weigh a person's heart to decide whether he or she deserved eternal life. Next, they used a kind of salt called natron, to dry the body out. The skin was preserved with resin, oil, and wax. The body was packed with linen or sawdust and finally wrapped in linen strips. Several nested cases held the body. Animals were preserved in the same way.

Freezing Up

Some mummies are naturally made when a body is quickly frozen. This is how Lyuba, Blue Babe, and Otzi became mummified. It's like putting a body in a freezer. Bodies that are frozen may be very well preserved, including the internal organs, blood, and other soft tissues. Once the bodies are removed from the ice, they begin to decay, so they must remain frozen.

Mummy Sequencing

Put these mummies in order from oldest to most recent to unscramble the word.

T	Tamut	2,900 years ago
I	Otzi	5,300 years ago
R	Inca Maiden	500 years ago
H	Lyuba	42,000 years ago
S	King Tut	3,300 years ago
Y	Vladimir Lenin	about 100 years ago
O	Tollund Man	2,300-2,400 years ago

Fuzzy Dates

How can the Tollund Man be dated to 2,300-2,400 years ago? Did it take a hundred years for him to die? No!

Scientists have different ways of dating mummies and other historical artifacts. Some things are written down by historians at the time. We know Lenin's exact date of death, because we have historical records that talk about him and record his death.

But there were no people writing about the Tollund Man when he died. So scientists use clues to learn when he died. They look at the soil around him, at the mummy itself, and at any artifacts found near the mummy.

If you found a mummy holding an iron sword, you might not know *exactly* when that mummy lived, but you could make an educated guess. The mummy had to live sometime after people learned how to make things out of iron.

These clues help scientists come up with a range of time. They can be confident that the mummy comes from some time within that range. The Tollund Man could be as old as 2,400 years old, or as recent as 2,300 years. But we know he's from around that time period.

Answer: HISTORY

Natural or Not?

Some mummies are formed by nature. Other mummies are preserved because people worked hard to make sure the body would be protected. Sort the following mummies based on whether they are natural or man-made.

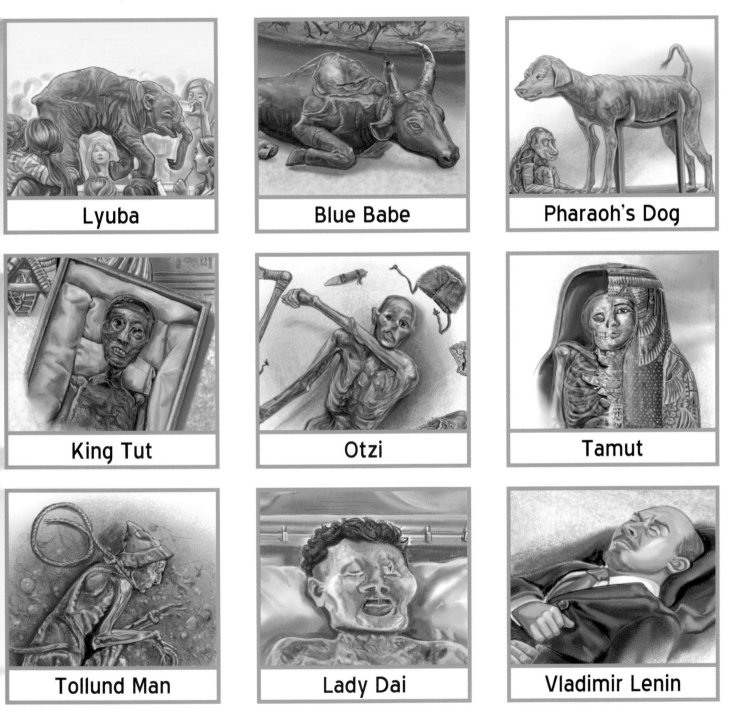

Lyuba

Blue Babe

Pharaoh's Dog

King Tut

Otzi

Tamut

Tollund Man

Lady Dai

Vladimir Lenin

Natural: Lyuba, Blue Babe, Otzi, Tollund Man
Man-made: King Tut, Pharaoh's Dog, Tamut, Lady Dai, Vladimir Lenin

Thanks to the following individuals for verifying the accuracy of the information in this book.
· Dr. Johan Reinhard, currently an Explorer with National Geographic Society
· Dr. Salima Ikram, Distinguished University Professor of Egyptology at The American University in Cairo
· Dr. Randall Thompson, HORUS Group

Library of Congress Cataloging-in-Publication Data

Names: Donald, Rhonda Lucas, 1962- author. | Morrison, Cathy, illustrator.
Title: If a mummy could talk ... / by Rhonda Lucas Donald ; illustrated by
  Cathy Morrison.
Description: Mt. Pleasant, SC : Arbordale Publishing, [2019] | Audience: Ages
  4-9. | Audience: K to grade 3. | Includes bibliographical references.
Identifiers: LCCN 2018040511 (print) | LCCN 2018041337 (ebook) | ISBN
  9781607187554 (English PDF) | ISBN 9781643511559 (English ePub) | ISBN
  9781607187677 (Interactive, read-aloud ebook English) | ISBN
  9781607187370 (english hardcover) | ISBN 9781607187431 (english pbk.) |
  ISBN 9781607187486 (spanish pbk.)
Subjects: LCSH: Mummies--Juvenile literature. | Mummified animals--Juvenile
  literature. | Human remains (Archaeology)--Juvenile literature. | Animal
  remains (Archaeology)--Juvenile literature.
Classification: LCC GT3340 (ebook) | LCC GT3340 .D66 2019 (print) | DDC
  393/.3--dc23
LC record available at https://lccn.loc.gov/2018040511

Lexile® Level: 630L
key phrases: science & technology, archaeology, archaeologists, paleontologists, mummy, mummified animals

Bibliography:
 "Ancient Mummy Shows Person Had Lung Infection at Time of Death." Popular Archaeology. 25 July 2012.
    Web. 8 Nov. 2017.
"Bon Anniversaire, Blue Babe." Museum of the North. Museum of the North, July 2014. Web. 8 Nov. 2017.
Bonn-Muller, Eti. "China's Sleeping Beauty." Archaeology Archive. Archaeology.org, 10 Apr. 2009. Web. 8 Nov.
    2017.
Gannon, Megan. "Mummy Murder Mystery: King Ramesses III Throat Slashed." Live Science. Live Science, 18
    Dec. 2012. Web. 8 Nov. 2017.
Hsu, Jeremy. "Lenin's Body Improves with Age." Scientific American. Scientific American, 22 Apr. 2015. Web. 8
    Nov. 2017.
Nine to Noon. "Salima Ikram: Animal Mummy Project." Radio New Zealand, 11 Dec. 2015. Web. 8 Nov. 2017.
Macrae, Fiona. "Unraveled After 3,000 Years, the Secrets of the Singing Mummy." Science & Tech. Daily Mail, 9
    Apr. 2014. Web. 8 Nov. 2017.
"Mummies: Newborn Siberian Woolly Mammoths Yield Trove of Insights." Scientific Computing. American
    Museum of Natural History, 9 July 2014. Web. 8 Nov. 2017.
"Otzi the Iceman." South Tyrol Museum of Archaeology, 2016. Web. 8 Nov. 2017.
Veldmeijer, Andre. "King Tut Wore Orthopedic Sandals." Seeker. Discovery Communications, 7 Apr. 2010. Web.
    8 Nov. 2017.
The Tollund Man: A Face from Prehistoric Denmark. Museum Silkeborg, 2004. Web. 8 Nov. 2017.

Manufactured in China, December 2018
This product conforms to CPSIA 2008
First Printing

Arbordale Publishing
Mt. Pleasant, SC 29464
www.ArbordalePublishing.com